DISCOVERING GEOGRAPHY

STATES

DAVID L. STIENECKER

■

ART BY RICHARD MACCABE

BENCHMARK BOOKS

MARSHALL CAVENDISH

NEW YORK

Benchmark Books
Marshall Cavendish Corporation
99 White Plains Road
Tarrytown, New York 10591

©Marshall Cavendish Corporation, 1998

Series created by Blackbirch Graphics, Inc.

Printed and bound in the United States.

Library of Congress Cataloging-in-Publication Data

Stienecker, David.
　　States / by David L. Stienecker.
　　　　p.　　cm. — (Discovering geography)
　　Includes index.
　　Summary: Examines the geography of the United States
through a series of maps which illustrate particular aspects of
the country and provides follow-up questions and activities
for further study.
　　ISBN 0-7614-0541-0 (lib. bdg.)
　　1. United States—Geography—Juvenile literature.
[1. United States—Geography. 2. Geography.] I. Title.
II. Series: Discovering Geography (New York, N.Y.)
E161.3.S75　　1998
917.3—dc21
　　　　　　　　　　　　　　　　　　　　　　　　　　97-2071
　　　　　　　　　　　　　　　　　　　　　　　　　　CIP
　　　　　　　　　　　　　　　　　　　　　　　　　　AC

Contents

■■■■■■■

Then and Now

This map shows what the United States looked like in 1776. The thirteen colonies made up the total area of the United States.

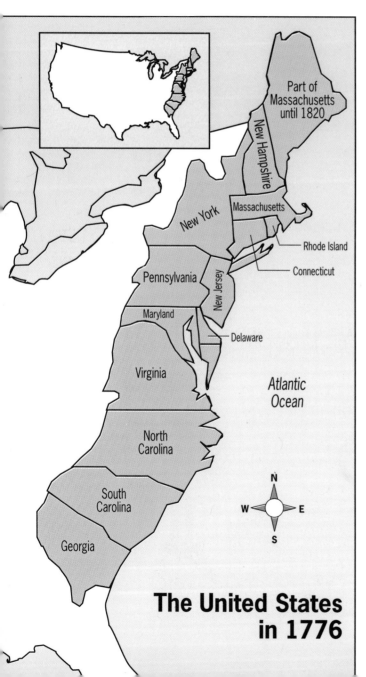

The United States in 1776

- What are the names of the thirteen colonies? What color is used to show them?

- Which colony was the farthest north? Which was the farthest south?

- How would you describe the location of the territory of the United States in 1776?

The map on page 5 shows what the United States looks like today. The dates tell which year each state officially became a state.

Use the maps on these pages to play a game of "Then and Now." Each player should write four questions on index cards, one question per card.

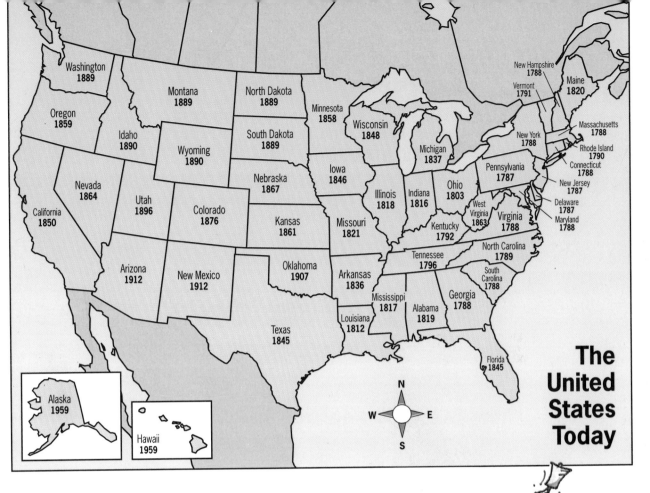

The United States Today

You should be able to answer each question by using the maps. Here are some examples:

- In which years did New Hampshire, New Jersey, and North Carolina officially become states?

- In which direction did the United States expand?

Turn the cards over and mix them up. Each player in turn draws a card and answers the question. If the player gives the wrong answer, the card is returned to the pile. The player who answers the most questions wins.

The thirteen colonies became the original thirteen states.

Region by Region

The United States can be divided into six regions.
Look at the map to discover what they are.

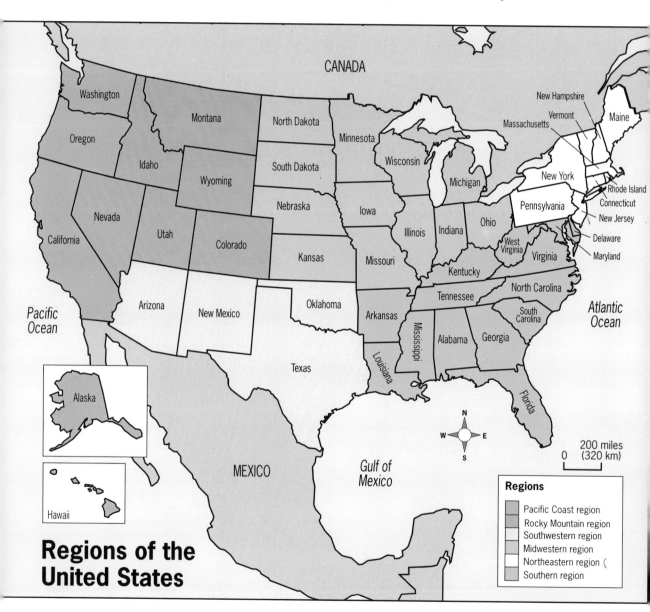

Regions of the United States

Regions:
- Pacific Coast region
- Rocky Mountain region
- Southwestern region
- Midwestern region
- Northeastern region
- Southern region

• How do you think each region got its name?

- Make a chart like this one to show which states are in each region.

Region	State

Add the name of the region your state is in to your chart.

- Use the map to answer these region riddles.

I'm the largest state in the Southwestern region. Part of me borders Mexico and part of me borders the Gulf of Mexico. What state am I?

I'm the northernmost state in the continental United States. What state am I? What region am I in?

My state is a peninsula in the Gulf of Mexico. What state am I? What region am I in?

Most of my northern Rocky Mountain region border shares a border with Canada. What state am I?

Make up some region riddles of your own. Give them to a friend along with the map to solve.

You can use the map key to help you identify different kinds of terrain.

What's the Land Like?

If you want to know what the land is like, look at a terrain map. A terrain map shows different kinds of geographical features such as mountains, hills, plateaus, and plains. This is a terrain map of Alaska.

- What kind of land runs along the north coast of Alaska? The west coast?

- What kind of land describes where Fairbanks is?

- On which coast are there plateaus and hills?

- Plan a trip across Alaska following the Yukon River. Begin on the west coast and travel as far east as you can. Describe the kind of land you would pass through as you travel from west to east.

- If you lived in Alaska's capital city of Juneau, what kind of land would you live on?

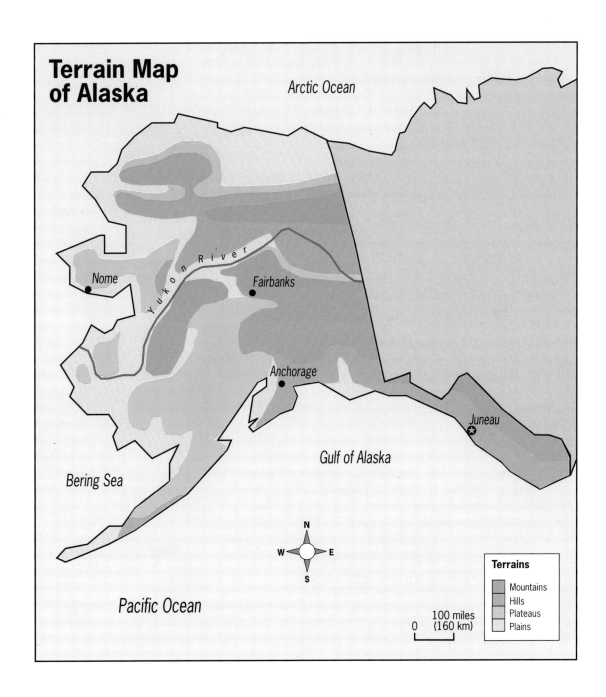

Terrain Map of Alaska

Arctic Ocean

Yukon River

Nome

Fairbanks

Anchorage

Juneau

Bering Sea

Gulf of Alaska

Pacific Ocean

N
W E
S

100 miles
0   (160 km)

Terrains

- Mountains
- Hills
- Plateaus
- Plains

Hot, Cold, Wet, Dry

You can use maps to show average temperatures of an area. This map shows average temperatures for the United States in the month of January. Different colors are used to show the average temperature in different parts of the country. Use the map key to find out what the colors stand for.

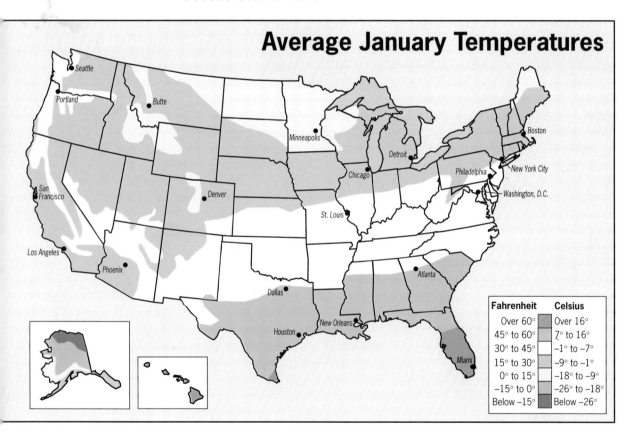

Average January Temperatures

Fahrenheit	Celsius
Over 60°	Over 16°
45° to 60°	7° to 16°
30° to 45°	−1° to −7°
15° to 30°	−9° to −1°
0° to 15°	−18° to −9°
−15° to 0°	−26° to −18°
Below −15°	Below −26°

- Which parts of the United States have mild winters?

- What are the average January temperatures for your state? What is the average yearly precipitation?

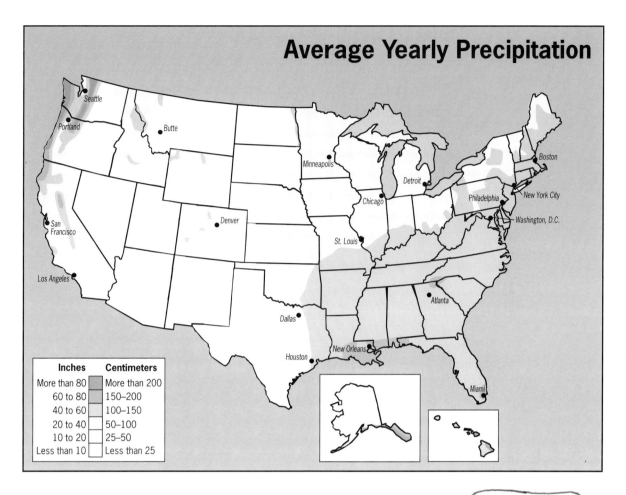

Average Yearly Precipitation

Inches	Centimeters
More than 80	More than 200
60 to 80	150–200
40 to 60	100–150
20 to 40	50–100
10 to 20	25–50
Less than 10	Less than 25

This is a precipitation map of the United States. It shows the average yearly precipitation for different parts of the country.

- Which parts of the United States have the most precipitation? Which part is the driest?

- Does the amount of precipitation increase or decrease as you travel from east to west? How can you tell?

Pick a state you would like to visit. Then use the maps to decide the best time of year to go there.

Precipitation is the amount of rain, snow, or sleet that falls to Earth.

Natural Landmarks

The United States has many beautiful natural landmarks. They include huge forests, rugged mountains, and deep canyons. Millions of people visit these places every year. This map shows some of them. There are many more.

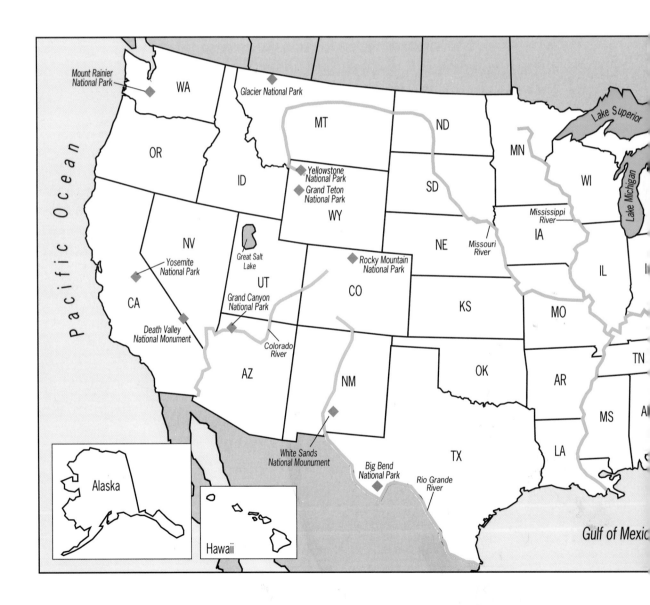

• Turn back to the "Regions of the United States" map on page 6. Use it and this map to make a chart of landmarks like this one:

Region	Natural Landmarks
Pacific Coast	Yosemite National Park, Mount Rainier National Park

More than 2 million people visit Yellowstone National Park each year!

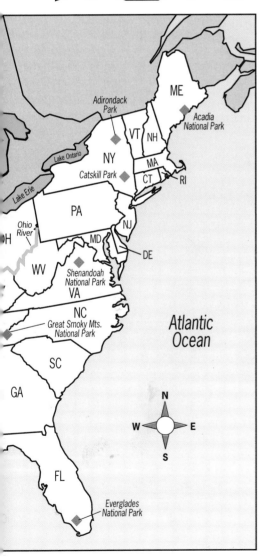

• To what state would you travel to visit Acadia National Park?

• What national park lies along the Colorado River?

• When visiting Yellowstone National Park, what other park could you easily travel to?

• Plan a cross-country trip to visit as many natural landmarks as you can. Write up your trip and share it with others.

Parts of the Grand Canyon are a mile (1.6 km) deep and 18 miles (29 km) across! It has been called the grandest of all canyons.

How Many People?

If you want to know how many people live in a certain part of the United States, you can use a population map. The map uses colors to show population densities. You can use the map to come to some interesting conclusions.

- Is the population greater in the eastern half or the western half of Maine?

- Which states have population densities of over 260 people per square mile (670 per sq. km)?

- What is the population density of most of Vermont?

- If you lived on Cape Cod in Massachusetts, what would the population density be?

- If you traveled through Massachusetts north from Springfield, which population densities would you find?

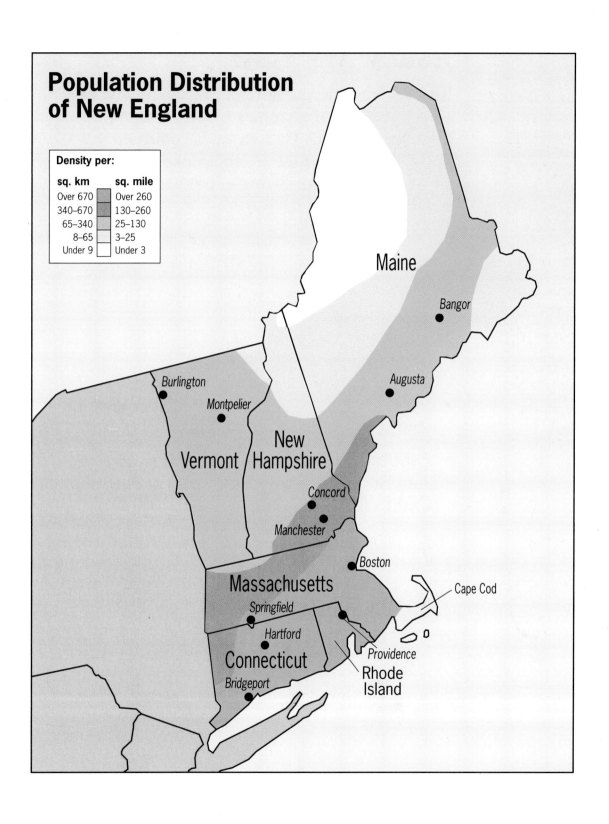

Population Distribution of New England

Density per:

sq. km	sq. mile
Over 670	Over 260
340–670	130–260
65–340	25–130
8–65	3–25
Under 9	Under 3

Maine

Bangor

Burlington

Augusta

Montpelier

New Hampshire

Vermont

Concord

Manchester

Boston

Massachusetts

Cape Cod

Springfield

Hartford

Providence

Connecticut

Rhode Island

Bridgeport

Follow the Flow

The map below shows some of the major rivers that criss-cross the continental United States. In the early 1800s, rivers were the main means of transporation. Today, rivers play an important role in shipping, irrigation, recreation, and as a source of food. Do any of these rivers pass through your state?

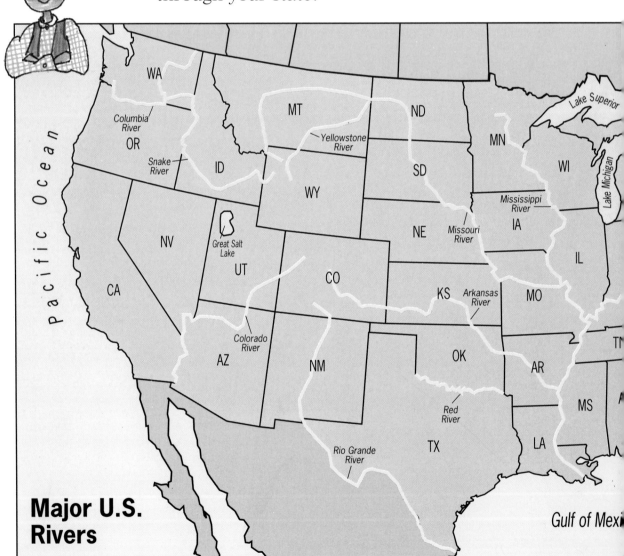

Major U.S. Rivers

- Locate the Mississippi River at its source in the northern state of Minnesota. Use your finger to trace the river across the United States to the Gulf of Mexico. Make a list of all the states it passes through.

- Now trace the route of the Missouri River. What states does it pass through?

- See if you can find a river route from the Mississippi River to the west coast of the United States.

The Mississippi River is the longest river in the United States. It flows for some 2,350 miles (3,780 km).

- Rivers often form state borders. Which states on the map have rivers for borders?

- What river flows from the Missouri River?

- What two rivers in the northwest are connected?

- Do some research to find out what rivers pass through your state. Then make a poster to show where the rivers flow.

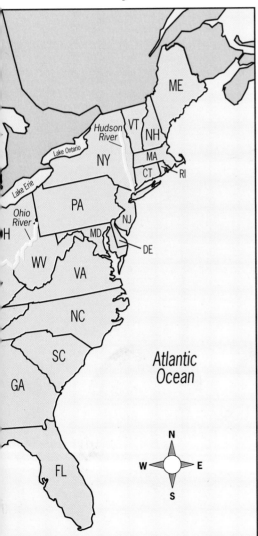

ME

Hudson River
VT
NH
Lake Ontario
NY
MA
CT
RI

Lake Erie
PA
Ohio River
NJ
H
MD
DE
WV
VA
NC
SC
Atlantic Ocean
GA
FL

N
W E
S

17

This is what the symbol for an interstate looks like.

Highways Across America

The United States has a federal highway system. Its official name is the National System of Interstate and Defense Highways. But most people simply call them "interstate highways."

Interstate highways connect 90 percent of all the cities in the United States with populations over 50,000. Look at this map of four states that are connected by interstate highways.

- Find the interstate highways that will take you from San Diego, California, to Tucson, Arizona.

- What interstate highway would you use to travel from Salt Lake City, Utah, to San Diego, California?

- Find the interstate highway that will take you through the state of Nevada.

Interstate highways with even numbers run east and west. Highways with odd numbers run north and south.

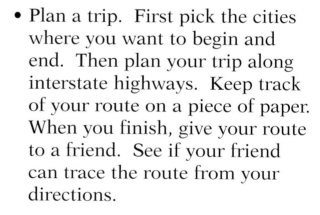

- Plan a trip. First pick the cities where you want to begin and end. Then plan your trip along interstate highways. Keep track of your route on a piece of paper. When you finish, give your route to a friend. See if your friend can trace the route from your directions.

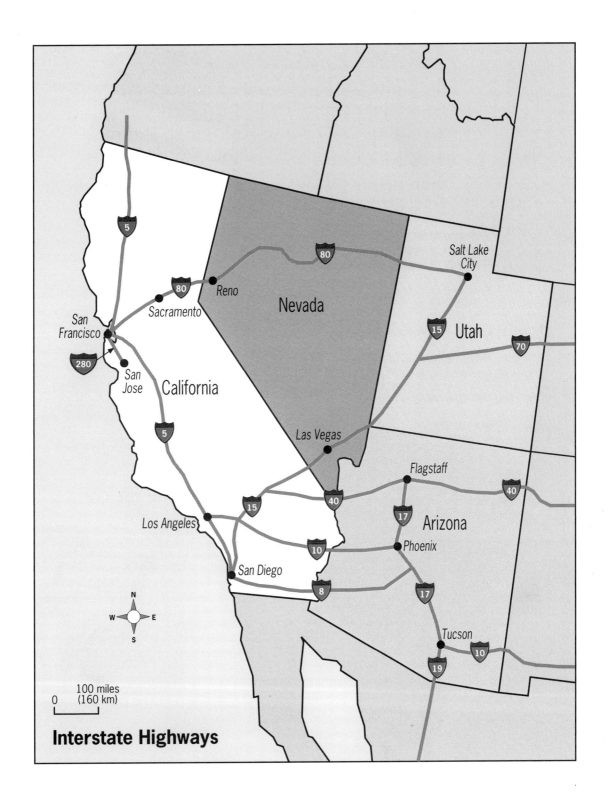

Interstate Highways

Off the Beaten Path

At first, this map of New York State may look a little confusing. It is a road map like one you might use on a trip. But it shows more than interstate highways. It also shows U.S. highways and state highways. Just look at the map key to find the symbols.

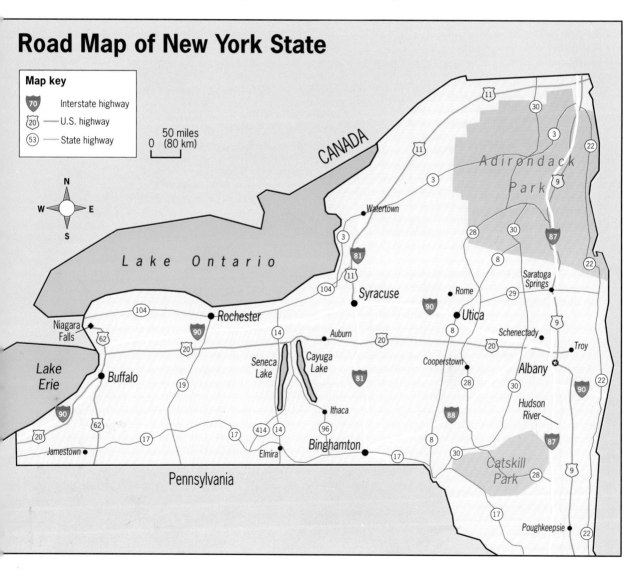

Road Map of New York State

Map key

- 70   Interstate highway
- 20   U.S. highway
- 53   State highway

50 miles
0   (80 km)

Very often the most interesting places to visit and see are off the interstate highways. To get to them you must take other roads.

- Interstate highway 87 passes through Adirondack Park. But if you really wanted to explore the park, you would have to take some state highways. Plan a trip around and through Adirondack Park on state highways. Write a travel guide for someone to follow.

- See if you can find these interesting places on the map. Just follow the directions.

  Follow Interstate 88 until you reach State highway 28. Take highway 28 north to Cooperstown. Here you can visit the National Baseball Hall of Fame and Museum.

  Look along Interstate 87 until you find State highway 29. If you get off here, you can visit Saratoga Springs. Saratoga Springs is a famous health resort. It is also where the potato chip was invented.

  Find Seneca Lake on the map. It's a long skinny lake. What highways would you take if you wanted to drive around the lake?

- Find out what highways other than interstate highways are near you. Make a map to show where they are. Find out if there are some interesting places to see along the highways.

Capital Hop

Every state has a capital city. The capital city is where the state government is located. It is where elected state officials have their offices and work. This map shows the names and locations of state capitals. Use the map key to help you locate them.

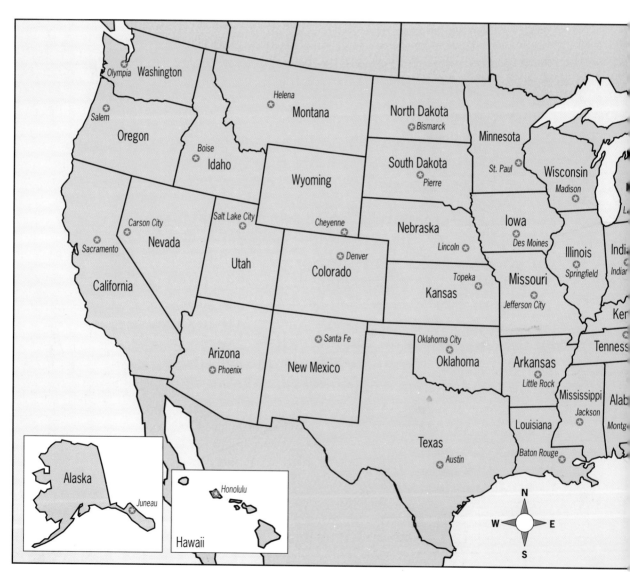

- Locate your state and its capital city. Locate the capital cities of the surrounding states.

- Use the map scale to estimate the distance from your capital city to the capital cities of surrounding states.

- The United States has a capital city, too. It is usually referred to as "The Capital of the United States." Find it on the map. Use the map key to help you. Use the map scale to estimate the distance from your capital city to the capital of the United States.

- Plan a trip across the United States, hopping from one capital city to another. Give a list of the state capitals to a friend or partner—don't give them the names of the states. Have your partner trace your route from capital city to capital city, naming the states as they go.

A star symbol is used to show a capital city.

Washington, D.C., is the capital of the United States and home to our nation's government.

Capital Cities

New Hampshire
Vermont
Montpelier
Maine
Augusta
Concord
Albany
New York
Boston
Massachusetts
Providence
Rhode Island
Hartford
Connecticut
New Jersey
Pennsylvania
Harrisburg
Trenton
Delaware
Dover
hio
West Virginia
mbus
Richmond
Maryland
Annapolis
fort Charleston
Virginia
Washington, D.C.
Raleigh
North Carolina
Columbia South Carolina
Atlanta
Georgia
Tallahassee
Florida

★ National capital
✪ Capital city

150 miles
(240 km)
0

How is the Land Used?

You can use a map to find out how people use the land. These special maps are called "Land Use Maps." This map shows how land is used in California.

- How can you tell from the map if the land is used mainly for grazing? For farmland? As a manufacturing center?

- Which part of California is mostly forest land? Which part is mostly farmland?

- Imagine you are traveling by car from San Francisco to San Diego. Describe the different ways the land is used as you travel through the state.

- What kind of land lies along the coast of California between San Francisco and Oakland?

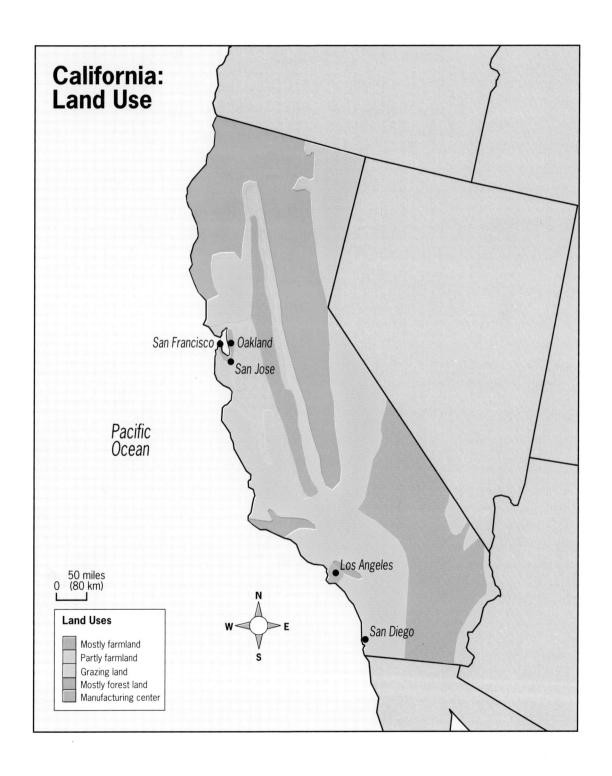

California:
Land Use

Pacific
Ocean

San Francisco ● ● Oakland
● San Jose

● Los Angeles

● San Diego

50 miles
0 (80 km)

N
W ● E
S

Land Uses

Mostly farmland
Partly farmland
Grazing land
Mostly forest land
Manufacturing center

Hawaii became the 50th state on August 21, 1959.

Distant States

There are two states that are not connected to the continental United States. They are Alaska and Hawaii.

This is a map of Hawaii. Hawaii lies about 2,400 miles (3,860 km) southwest of San Francisco, California, in the Pacific Ocean. It is the only state that does not lie on the North American continent. It is also the only state made up of islands. This map of Hawaii shows the states eight main islands.

- Become familiar with Hawaii. Play "Where Am I Now?" with a friend. Here's how:

    1. Pick a place on the map, but don't tell your partner what it is.

    2. Give your partner a clue to the location of your place. For example, the name of a nearby landmark or town.

    3. Keep giving clues until your partner guesses where you are. Then switch roles and play again. Play several rounds.

    4. Give one point for every clue. The winner is the player with the fewest points at the end of the game.

Hawaii is a chain of 132 volcanic islands.

Hawaii

25 miles
0 (40 km)

N
W ● E
S

Kauai
∧ Mt. Waialeale

Niihau

Oahu

Pearl City
Kaneohe
Kailua
Waipahu
Diamond Head
Pearl Harbor
Honolulu

Molokai

Wailuku
Kahului
Lanai
Maui
Haleakala
National Park

Kahoolawe

Pacific
Ocean

Hawaii

∧
Mauna Kea
Hilo
Kailua
Kona

∧
Mauna Loa
Hawaii Volcanoes
National Park

What's Made There?

This kind of map is called a product map. You can use maps like this to learn about the things that are made or produced in a state. What products does this map show?

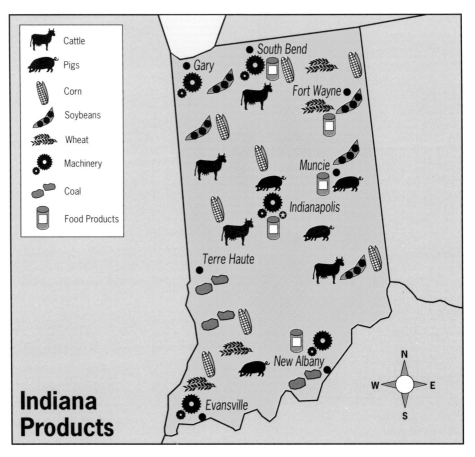

Indiana Products

- You can use a product map to see how people in a state earn a living. What are some ways people in Indiana earn a living?

- Make a product map of your state. Encyclopedias are a good place to find the information you need.

Answers

Pps. 4–5 Then and Now

The thirteen colonies were: Virginia, Massachusetts, New Hampshire, New York, Connecticut, Maryland, Rhode Island, Delaware, Pennsylvania, North Carolina, New Jersey, South Carolina, and Georgia. They are shown in the color orange.

New Hampshire was the farthest north. Georgia was the farthest south.

The territory of the United States in 1776 was a narrow strip of land along the eastern coast of North America.

The dates these colonies became states were: New Jersey–1787, New Hampshire–1788, North Carolina–1789.

The United States expanded to the west.

Pps. 6–7 Region by Region

The name of each region reflects its geographical location within the United States.

Chart answers should read:

Northeastern region: Maine, New Hampshire, Vermont, Massachusetts, Connecticut, Rhode Island, Pennsylvania, New York, New Jersey.

Southern region: Maryland, Virginia, Delaware, West Virginia, Kentucky, Tennessee, North Carolina, South Carolina, Arkansas, Louisiana, Mississippi, Alabama, Georgia, Florida.

Midwestern region: North Dakota, South Dakota, Minnesota, Wisconsin, Michigan, Ohio, Indiana, Illinois, Iowa, Missouri, Nebraska, Kansas.

Southwestern region: Oklahoma, Texas, New Mexico, Arizona.

Rocky Mountain region: Montana, Idaho, Wyoming, Colorado, Utah, Nevada.

Pacific Coast region: Washington, Oregon, California, Alaska, Hawaii.

Texas.

Maine is the northernmost state in the continental United States. It is in the Northeastern region.

Florida. It is in the Southern region.

Montana.

Pps. 8–9 What's the Land Like?

Plains run along the north and west coast of Alaska.

Fairbanks is in the mountains.

The southern coast has both plateaus and hills.

If you followed the Yukon River from west to east you would travel through plains first, pass by plateaus, then travel with mountains on the east, then travel through plateaus, and then through hills.

Juneau is in the hills.

Pps. 10–11 Hot, Cold, Wet, Dry

Hawaii and the southeastern, southern, and southwestern parts of the United States have mild winters.

The eastern and southern parts of the United States have the most precipitation. The southwestern part is the driest.

The colors on the map indicate that precipitation decreases from east to west.

Pps. 12–13 Natural Landmarks

Maine; Grand Canyon National Park; Grand Teton National Park.

Pps. 14–15 How Many People?

The eastern half of Maine.

Connecticut, Rhode Island, and Massachusetts.

It is 25–130 people per square mile (65–340 per sq. km).

Cape Cod has 3–25 people per square mile (8–65 per sq. km).

North from Springfield you would find densities per square mile of over 260 (670 sq. km), then 130–260 (340–670 sq. km), and then 25–130 (65–340 sq. km).

Pps. 16–17 Follow the Flow

The Mississippi River flows through: Minnesota, Wisconsin, Iowa, Illinois, Missouri, Arkansas, Kentucky, Tennessee, Mississippi, and Louisiana.

The Missouri River flows through: Missouri, Kansas, Iowa, Nebraska, South Dakota, North Dakota, Montana, and Wyoming.

On this map, rivers form borders between Washington and Oregon, Idaho and Washington, Idaho and Oregon, Texas and Mexico, Texas and Oklahoma, Nebraska and Iowa, Nebraska and South Dakota, Kansas and Missouri, Minnesota and Wisconsin, Iowa and Illinois, Missouri and Illinois, Missouri and Kentucky, Arkansas and Tennessee, Arkansas and Mississippi, Louisiana and Mississippi, Illinois and Kentucky, Indiana and Kentucky, Ohio and Kentucky, Ohio and West Virginia.

The Yellowstone River flows from the Missouri.

The Columbia and the Snake Rivers are connected.

Pps. 18–19 Highways Across America

Interstate 8, and then Interstate 17 will take you to Tucson.

From Salt Lake City to San Diego, you would take Interstate 15.

Interstate 80 will take you through Nevada.

Pps. 20–21 Off the Beaten Path

To drive around Seneca Lake, you would travel on State highways 14 and 414.

Pps. 22–23 Capital Hop

No answers.

Pps. 24–25 How is the Land Used?

Land used for grazing is colored orange. Land used for farming is colored dark brown, manufacturing centers are bright pink.

Forest land is found in the northwest and in a strip through the center. Farmland is found in the southeast, and in a strip west of the forest land.

From San Francisco to San Diego you would travel through farmland, grazing land, forest land, a manufacturing center, and more grazing land.

Manufacturing centers.

Pps. 26–27 Two Distant States

No answers.

P. 28 What's Made There?

Answers will vary.

Glossary

basin A region of land drained by a river and its branches.

border The boundary of a state or country.

capital city The city where the state government is located.

compass rose A diagram on a map that shows the direction of North, South, East, and West.

continental United States All of the United States except Alaska and Hawaii.

interstate highway A national highway that passes through more than one state.

locator map A small map that is used to identify the geographical location of an area shown on a larger map.

map key A list that explains the meaning of the symbols used on a map.

map scale A bar on a map used to calculate distance on the map.

plain A large flat stretch of land.

plateau A large and mostly flat area of raised land.

population center The point in a country around which the population is evenly balanced.

population density The average number of people who live in a given area.

precipitation Solid or liquid water that falls to Earth's surface, such as rain, snow, or sleet.

region Any large part of Earth's surface.

terrain The geographical or physical features of an area of land.

Index